Preface:

    While we go to testing of the software that is being developed we will use testing tools. These are of two kinds manual testing and Automated testing. In manual testing each and every step is tested and automated testing the same is done by software. Quick test professional (QTP) developed by HP is an automated testing tool. It is very popular and used in almost every software development company at there quality and testing department. This book is a lecturer notes which was by an experienced lecturer. The book is written as it is. Hope you like the book.

    Thank you

Quick Test Professional (QTP)

25

25th July,2013

> Tips for generating the basic Vb script for windows based applications.

Winobjec Script

*Dialog
   Dialog("Dialog Name")

*Window
   Window("Window Name")

*TextBox/EditBox
   WinEdit("EditBoxName")

*ComboBox/ListBox
   WinListBox("ListBoxName")

*CheckBox
   WinCheckBox("CheckBoxName")

*WinButton/PsuhButton
   WinButton("ButtonName")

*RadioButton
   WinRadioButton("RadioButtonName")

Operation\UserAction   Script

*Invoke

2

Activate

*Enter a value in the text box "Value/Text"	Set
*RadioButton	Set
*CheckBox	Set On/Off
*Button	Click
*ListBox/ComboBox "Item/No"	Select
*Password "*******"	SetSecure

Develop the Vb Script for login operation

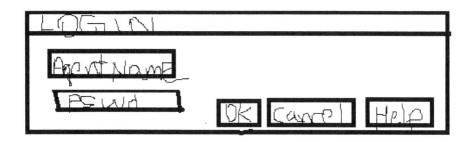

Dialaog("Login").Activate

Dialog("Login").WinEdit("AgentName").Set "Roopa"

Dialog("Login").WinEdit("Password").SetSecure "******"

Dialog("Login").WinButton("OK").Click

Window("Flight Reservation").Close

➢ How many ways of functional testing?

1. Manual Testing and
2. Automation Testing

1. **Manual Testing :** Manual Testing is a process in which all the phases of Software Testing Life Cycle like
    a. Test Planning
    b. Test Development
    c. Test Execution
    d. Result Analysis
    e. Bug Tracking and Reporting are accomplished successfully manual with human efforts.

➢ Drawbacks:
    1. More number of people are required.
    2. Time consuming.
    3. No accuracy (or) Human errors.
    4. Tiredness.
    5. Can't repeat the tasks easily.
    6. Repeated actions are not possible.

2. **Automation Testing**: It is a process in which all the drawbacks of manual testing are addressed properly and provides speed and accuracy to the existing testing process.

➢ Drawbacks:
    1. Costly tool
    2. All the areas can't be automated.

➢ Types of Automated Tool:
Automated tools can be broadly divided into 3 types:
    1. Functional Tools: QTP,Selenium,Win Runner,…

4

2. Management Tools: QC,Test Director,...
3. Performance Tools: Load Runner,Silk Performer,...

➢ QTP Introduction:

1. Types of the tool: Functional Tool.
2. Company: Taken by Mercury corporation and handled by HP.
3. Versions: 5.5,6.5,7.6,8.0,8.2,9.0,9.2,9.5,10.0,11.0 (latest 11.5 beta)
4. Scripting languages: VB Script/Java Script.

➢ Add-in Manager: It is provided by the QTP,if you want to enter QTP, we need to select anyone of the Add-in based on application.By default, its having three types of Add-in

ActiveX and visual basic for windows based applications.

Web for web based applications.

➢ Object Repository: It is a storage place. The properties and values will be stored under object repository. It can be divided into two types.

1. Local Repository.
2. Shared Repository.

1. Local Repository: By default, all the properties and values will be stored under local repositories.
   NOTE1: Local repository extension .mtr (mercury test repository)
   NOTE2: Shared repository extension .tsr (test share repository).
   NOTE3: We can modify local repository, but we cannot modify shared repository.
   NOTE4: Local repositories we cannot associate for multiple test and for shared repositories we can associate.

➢ Navigation for creating the shared repositories:

1. Go to the object repository, activate the file menu. Select the option, export local objects, specify the file name with the extension .tsr.
2. Go to the object repositories, tools menu, select the option associate repositories, the associate repositories which cannot be opened, click on add repository button and select the required .tsr file and select the available actions, click on associate button, click on OK.

   NOTE1: Above 2nd paragraph is for, only if any local repositories files are deleted)

   Shortcut key: object repository (ctrl + R)

Vb Script for CALC

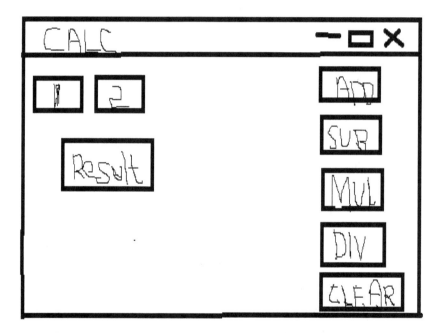

1. VbWindow("FORM1").vbEdit("TEST1").Set"1"
2. Vb Window("FORM1").VbEdit("TEXT2").Set"2"
3. VbWindow("FORM1").VbButton("ADD").Click
4. VbWindow("FORM1").VbButton("SUB").Click
5. VbWindow("FORM1").VbButton("MUL").Click

6. VbWindow("FORM1").VbButton("DIV").Click
7. VbWindow("FORM1").VbButton("CLEAR").Click
8. VbWindow("FORM1").Close

Utility Objects:

1.Invoke aapplication (or) Systemutil.Run:

➢ Invoke application is used to opening the application by QTP itself.

Syntax: Invokeapplication "Application Path"

(or)

SystemUtil.Run "Application Path"

2.RepositoriesCollection.Addmethod:

➢ To share the add repositories during the execution.

Syntax: RepositoriesCollection.Add "Path of the TSR file".

3.RepositoriesCollection.Remove:

➢ This utility option is used to remove on a specific repository file.

Syntax: RepositoriesCollection.Remove "Path of the TSR file".

4.RepositoriesCollection.RemoveAll:

➢ To remove all the repository files during the execution.

Syntax: RepositoriesCollection.RemoveAll

5.Reporter.Reporting:

> This utility is used to specifying the user defined result in the result name.

6.CaptureBitMap method:

> It is used to capture the specific object from the application.

Syntax: Objecthierarchy.CaptureBitMap "Path of the location file name with the extension.BMP"

4th Aug, 2013

QTP LifeCycle:

It contains 6 phases:

1. Test Planning.
2. Generating the basic Script.
3. Enhancing the test.
4. Debugging the test.
5. Executing the test.
6. Analyzing the result.

1. Test Planning: In this phase the automation test lead will do the following.

1. Understand the requirements.

2. Identifying the areas to be automated.

3. Analyzing the both positive and negative flow of the application.

4. Based on the above analysis he will prepare the automation test plan document.

5. He will prepare the tool ready for the operations with all the pre configurational settings.

2. Generating the basic Script: In this phase the automation test engineer will generate the basic test for both positive and negative flow of the application.

3.Enhancing the Test:

1. Data Driven Test with parameterization:

DDT: It is a concept provided in Automation inorder to implement retesting.

Steps to be followed to perform DDT.

1.Collects the data into the data table.

2.Generate the basic test.

3.Parameterize the test.

4.Execute the test.

5.Analyse the result.

2. Parameterization: It is a process of replacing the constants with the variables or parameters inorder to increase the scope of the test.

It can be done in 6 ways:

1.Through Data Driven Wizard.

2.Through Keyword view.

3.Manually.

4.Flat Files, Databases and Excel files(Adv. QTP).

5.Passing the input and output parameters.

6.Passing the input values during execution.

7.Declaring User Defined Variavles.

1.Through Data Driven Wizard:

Navigation:

1.Generating the basic script.

2.Collect the data into the data table.

3.Go to the Keyword view.

4.Select the constant value.

5.Click on configuration button.

6.Value configuration Wizard will be opened.

7.Select the option parameter.

8.Select the variable name.

9.Select the sheet as Global Sheet and click on OK.

Syntax: Datatable("Variable Name", Sheet Type)

Example:

Invokeapplication "C;\Programfiles\HP\QTP\Flight\app\Flight4a.exe"

Dialog("Login").Activate

Dialog("Login").WinEdit("AgentName:").Set Datatable("un", dtGlobalSheet)

Dialog("Login").WinEdit("Password:").SetSecure Datatable("pswd", dtGlobalSheet)

Dialog("Login").WinButton("OK").Click

Window("Flight Reservation").Close

6.Passing the input values during the execution:

Example:

Dim i,n,v1,v2

 n= inputbox("Enter number of iterations:")

for I = 1 to n

v1= inputbox("Enter the value v1:")

VbWindow("Form1").VbEdit("Text1").set v1

V2= inputbox("Enter the value v2:")

VbWindow("Form1").VbEdit("Test2").Set v2

VbWindow("FORM1").VbButton("ADD").Click

VbWindow("FORM1").VbButton("SUB").Click

VbWindow("FORM1").VbButton("MUL").Click

VbWindow("FORM1").VbButton("DIV").Click

VbWindow("FORM1").VbButton("CLEAR").Click

NOTE1:

GetItemCount Property: It is used to count the number of objects.

GetItem Property: It is used to capture the object name.

Example:

Count the number of objects on a desktop and capture those object names.

```
Dim i,n,Oname

n= Window("Program
Manager").WinListView("SysListView32").GetItemsCount()

msg box n

for i = 1 to n-1

Oname= Window("Program
Manager").WinListView("SysListView32").GetItem(i)

print(Oname)

Next
```

Example:

Count the number of objects on a tabbed window and capture those objects names.

```
Dim i,n,Oname

n= Dialog("Local Disk(D):
Properties").WinTab("SysTabControl32").GetItemsCount()

for i = 0 to n-1

Oname= Dialog("Local Disk(D):
Properties").WinTab("SysTabControl32").GetItem(i)

print(Oname)

Next
```

5th Aug,2013

NOTE:

GetRO Property: It is used to capture the actual value during the execution.

GetVisible Text: It is used to capture the static contents from the application.

Example of GetRO Property:

Dim res1,res2,res3,a,,b,c

VbWindow("Form1").VbEdit("Text1").Set parameter("V1")

VbWindow("Form1").VbEdit("Text2").Set parameter("V2")

VbWindow("Form1").VbButton("ADD").Click

res1= VbWindow("Form1").VbEdit("text3").GetROproperty("Text")

msgbox res1

VbWindow("Form1").VbButton("SUB").Click

res2= VbWindow("Form1").VbEdit("text3").GetROproperty("Text")

msgbox res2

VbWindow("Form1").VbButton("MUL").Click

res3= VbWindow("Form1").VbEdit("text3").GetROproperty("Text")

msgbox res3

Example for GetVisibleText:

result= Dialog("Login").GetVisibleText

msgbox result

Scenario: Do the parameterization for Flight Reservation window and capture order no. and confirmation message.

NOTE: Parameterization using keyword view method and capture the result using GetRO Property.

Example:

Window("Flight Reservation").Activate

Window("Flight Reservation").ActiveX("MaskEdBox").Type "121420"

Window("Flight Reservation").WinComboBox("FlyFrom:").Select "Denver"

Window("Flight Reservation").WinComboBox("Fly To:").Select "London"

Window("Flight Reservation").WinButton("Flight").Click

Window("Flight Reservation").Dialog("Flights Table").WinButton("Ok").Click

Window("Flight Reservation).Activate

Window("Flight Reservation").WinEdit("Name:").Set "roopa"

Window("Flight Reservation").WinButton("Insert Order").Click

14

Wait(7)

result= Window("Flight Reservation").WinEdit("Order No:").GetROProperty("Text")

msgbox result

result1= Window("Flight Reservation").ActiveX("ThreedPanelControl").GetROProperty("Text")

msgbox result1

Window("Flight Reservation").Active

Window("Flight Reservation").WinButton("Button").Click

Check Points:

QTP has provided 7 types of check points:

1. Standard Chechpoint.
2. Text Checkpoint.
3. Text Area Checkpoint.
4. Bitmap Checkpoint.
5. Database Checkpoint.
6. XML Checkpoint.
7. Accessibility Checkpoint.

NOTE: First 6 checkpoints are windows based checkpoint and last one is web based checkpoint.

1. **Standard Checkpoint:** It is used to capturing the actual value, and comparing the expected value with the actual value, if

expected value is equal to actual value result pass, otherwise result fail.

2. **Text Checkpoint:** It is used for checking the text present on a specified object.
3. **Text Area Checkpoint:** It is used for checking the text present on a specified area.
4. **Bitmap Checkpoint:** It is used to capturing the actual Bitmap and comparing the actual Bitmap With the expected Bitmap.

NOTE: Bitmap Checkpoint is used to compare the total Bitmap or part of a Bitmap.

5. **Database Checkpoint:** It is used to checking the content of a database

Navigation for inserting Database Checkpoint:

1.Activate the menu item insert.

2.Select the checkpoint type as Database Checkpoint.

3.Select the option specify SQL statement manually.

4.Click on Next button.

5.The database query wizard will be opened.

6.Click on create button to create the new connection string.

7.The database wizard will be opened.

8.Click on new button.

9.Select the database type.

10.Click on next.

11.Click on browse button and specify the data source name.

12.Save ODBC Microsoft Access Setup Wizard will be opened.

13.Select the Database, click on ok.

14.Now select the data source name.

15.Now specify the SQL statement.

16.Select SQL statement Select *from tablename

17.Click on OK.

6. **XML Checkpoint:** XML checkpoint is used to checking the content of the XML.
7. **Accessibility Checkpoint:** It is a web based checkpoint, it is used for checking whether the application is developed as per "www" standards.

Output Values: Capturing something during execution, we can findout result in the runtime data table, QTP has provided 4 types of output values

1. **Standard Output:** It is used for capturing the specific object properties and values.
2. **Database Output:** It is used to capturing the contents from the datatable.
3. **XML Output:** It is used to capturing the content from the XML file.
4. **Text Output:** It is used for checking the text present on a specified object.
5. **Text Area Output:** It is used for checking the text present in a specified area.

Example for Standard Output Value:

VbWindow("Form"1).VbButton("ADD").Output CheckPoint("ADD")

Example for Database Output:

DbTable("DbTable").Output CheckPoint("DbTable")

Example for XML Output Value:

XML File("cal.xml").Output CheckPoint("cal.xml")

Example for Text Output:

VbWindow("Form1").VbButton("Clear").Output CheckPoint("clear")

Example for Text Area Value:

VbWindow("Form1").Output CheckPoint("Form1")

Parameterization:

Environmental Variables: QTP has provided 2 types of environment variables.

1. User Defined Variables.
2. Built-in Variables.

Syntax: Environment.Value("Variable Name")

1.User Defined Variable: Replacing the constant value with a user defined variable.

NOTE:

Extention of the environment variable in >xml fies

Example:

VbWindow("Form1").VbEdit("Text1").Set Environment.Value("V1")

VbWindow("Form1").VbEdit("Text2").Set Environment Value("V2")

18

VbWindow("Form1").VbButton("ADD").Click

VbWindow("Form1").VbButton("CLEAR").Click

Navigation:

1.Activating menu item file.

2.Settings

3.Select the tab environment.

4.Select variable type as user defined.

5.Click on '+' configuration button.

6.The Add nNew Environment Parameter Wizard will be opened.

7.Specify the name and the value.

8.Click on ok.

9.Click on Export to create the 'XML' file.

10.Apply and OK.

2.Built-in Variables: These are pre-defined variables, wherever we want in the middle of the script, directly we can this variables.

Example:

Dim res1,res2,res3,res4,res5

res1= Environment.Value("Local Host Name")

msgbox res1

res2= Environment.Value("OS")

msgbox res2

res3= Environment.Value("OS Version")

msgbox res3

res4= Environment.Value("Product Name")

msgbox res4

res5= Environment.Value("Product Ver")

msgbox res5

10/8/2013

<u>**Data table methods:**</u> These are used for performing the operations on the run-time data type.

NOTE:

Designtime datatable Sheet id1   Sheet id2
External Data table Sheet id3

1. Add Sheet: This method is used for adding an extra sheet to Runtime data table.

Syntax: Datatable.AddSheet "Sheetname"

2. Delete Sheet: This method is used for deleting a specified sheet from run time data table.

Syntax: Datatable.DeleteSheet "Sheetname"

3. Import: This method is used for importing the data present in XL files to the run time data table.

Syntax: Datatable.Import "Path of the XL file"

4. Import Sheet: It is used for importing a specified sheet of the data from the excel file to a specified sheet of data in the run time data table.

Syntax: Datatable.ImportSheet "Path of the excel file, SourceSheet id, DestinationSheet id"

5. Export: It is used for exporting the data present in the run time data table to a specified location.

Syntax: Datatable.Export "Path of the Excel file"

6. Export Sheet: It is used for exporting a specified sheet of the data from the run time data table to a specified location.

Syntax: Datatable.Export "Path of the Excel File", Sheet id to be exported.

7. SetCurrentRow: It is used for making the QTP focus on a specified Row.

Syntax: Datatable.SetCurrentRow(RowNumber)

8. SetNextRow: It is used for making the QTP focus on the Next Row of the currently focused row.

Syntax: Datatable.SetNextRow

9. SetPrevRow: It is used for making the QTP focus on the previous row of the currently focused row.

Syntax: Datatable.SetPrevRow

10. Value Method: Value method is used for getting a value from a specified sheet, specified column and currently focused row.

11. GetSheet: It is used for making the QTP focus on a specified sheet.

Syntax: Datatable.GetSheet(SheetID)

12. GetRowCount: It is used for getting the rowcount.

NOTE:

By default it will return the global sheet row count.

var = Datatable.GetRowCount

Example:

Datatable.AddSheet "roopa"

Datatable.ImportSheet "d:\td.xls",1,3

n= Datatable.GetSheet(3).GetRowCount(i)

VbWindow("Form1").VbEdit("Text1").Set Datatable.Value("V1",3)

VbWindow("Form1").VbEdit("Text2").Set Datatable.Value("V2",3)

VbWindow("Form1").VbButton("ADD").Click

Actual = VbWindow("Form1").VbEdit("Text3").GetROProperty("Text")

Expval = Datatable.Value("ev",3)

If Cint(Expval) = Cint(Actual) Then

Datatable.Value("res",3)= Pass

Else

Datatable.Value("res",3)= Fail

End if

Next

Datatable.ExportSheet "d☺td1.xls",3

Recovery Scenarios (Exceptional handling):

Whenever we are executing the application, may we face some problematic situations like

1. Problems related to the Pop-up window.
2. Problems related to the Object state.
3. Problems related to the TestRun error.
4. Problems related to the Application crash/

For that QTP has provided 4 types of trigger events.

1. Pop-up window trigger event.
2. Object state trigger event.
3. TestRun error trigger event.
4. Application crash trigger event.

NOTE: Extension of the recovery scenarios is .QRS(Quick Recovery Scenario).

Working with Databases:

NOTE:

ADODB: The ADO(Activates Data Objects) is used to create a connection to a data source. Through this connection we can access multiple databases.

NOTE:

ADODB.RecordSet: It is used to hold a set of records(tables) from the databases.

 NOTE:

MOVENEXT: This method is used to move current field to next field.

Example:

Dim Con,Rs

Set Con = CreateObject("ADODB.Connection")

Set Rs = CreateObject("ADODB.RecordSet")

Con.Provider = "Microsft.Jet.OleDb.4.0"

Con.Open = "d:\roops.mdb"

Rs.Open "Select * from cal",Con

Do While not Rs.EOF

VbWindow("Form1").VbEdit("text1").Set Rs.Fields("v1")

VbWindow("Form1").VbEdit("text2").Set Rs.Fields("v2")

VbWindow("Form1").VbButton("ADD").Click

VbWindow("Form1").VbButton("SUB").Click

VbWindow("Form1").VbButton("MUL").Click

VbWindow("Form1").VbButton("DIV").Click

VbWindow("Form1").VbButton("CLEAR").Click

Rs.MoveNext

Loop

<u>16/8/2013</u>

<u>Keyword Driven Frame Work:</u>

Dim Res

Res= Datatable.Value("Keys",1)

Select Case Res

Case "K1"

Call login()

Call insertorder()

Call openorder()

Call logout()

Case "K2"

Call login()

Call insertorder()

Call logout()

Case "K3"

Call login()

Call openorder()

Call logout()

Case "K4"

Call login()

Call logout()

End Select

18/8/2013

Working with Flat Files:

1.Write a program to read data from a text file.

NOTE:

OpenTextFile method: This method is used to opening an existing text file.

Syntax: .OpenTextFile "path of the txt file"

(1= read, 2=write)

ReadAll method: To read the complete data from the text file.

Example:

Dim Fso,F1

Set Fso = CreateObject("Scripting.FileSystemObject")

Set F1= Fso.OpenTextFile("c:\d and s|s1|desktop\1234.txt",1)

Msgbox ReadAll

2.Write a program to write data into a text.

NOTE:

CreateTextFile method: This method is used to creating a text file to a specific location.

Syntax: .CreateTextFile("txt file location")

WriteLine method: This method is used to write the data line by line.

Write method: This method is used to write the data character wise.

WriteBlankLines method: This method is used to write the blank lines.

Example:

Dim Fso,F1

Set Fso = CreateObject("Scripting.FileSystemObject")

Set F1 = Fso.CreateTextFile("c:\d and s\s1\Desktop\result.txt",2)

F1.Write("Good Morning")

F1.WriteBlankLines(10)

F1.WriteLine("How are you")

F1.WriteLine("Welcome to India")

a)Do the parameterization for flight reservation window through scripting (If the customer is provided the data in the flat file)

Step1: Prepare the test data in the following name.

D_flight@fly_from@fly_to@c-name

121222@London@Denver@roopa

121223@Denver@Paris@roopa1

Step2: Generating the basic script for flight reservation window.

Dim Fso,F,F1,arr

Set Fso = CreateObject("Scripting.FileSystemObject")

Set F1 = Fso.OpenTextFile("d:\testdata.Txt",1)

```
F1.SkipLine

Do While not F1.At End Of Stream = true

arr = F1.ReadLine

arr = split(arr,"@")

Window("Flight Reservation").Activate

Window("Flight Reservation").WinObject("Date of Flight:").Type arr(0)

Window("Flight Reservation").WinComboBox("Fly From:").Select arr(1)

Window("Flight Reservation").WinComboBox("Fly To:").Select arr(2)

Window("Flight Reservation").WinButton("Flight").Click

Window("Flight Reservation").Dialog("Flight
Table").WinButton("OK").Click

Window("Flight Reservation").Activate

Window("Flight Reservation").WinEdit("Name:").Set arr(3)

Window("Flight Reservation").WinButton("Insert Order").Click

Window("Flight Reservation").Activate

Window("Flight Reservation").WinButton("Button).Click

Loop
```

B)Capture the order number and write into an text file.

```
Dim Fso,F,F1,arr,Output
```

```
Set Fso = CreateObject("Scripting.FileSystemObject")

Set F1 = Fso.OpenTextFile("d:\testdata.Txt",1)

Set F = Fso.CreateTextFile("d:\result1.txt",2)

F1.SkipLine

Do While not F1.At End Of Stream = true

arr = F1.ReadLine

arr = split(arr,"@")

Window("Flight Reservation").Activate

Window("Flight Reservation").WinObject("Date of Flight:").Type arr(0)

Window("Flight Reservation").WinComboBox("Fly From:").Select arr(1)

Window("Flight Reservation").WinComboBox("Fly To:").Select arr(2)

Window("Flight Reservation").WinButton("Flight").Click

Window("Flight Reservation").Dialog("Flight
Table").WinButton("OK").Click

Window("Flight Reservation").Activate

Window("Flight Reservation").WinEdit("Name:").Set arr(3)

Window("Flight Reservation").WinButton("Insert Order").Click

Wait(10)
```

Output = Window("Flight Reservation").WinEdit("Order No:").GetROProperty("text")

F.WriteLine(Output)

Window("Flight Reservation").Activate

Window("Flight Reservation").WinButton("Button").Click

Loop

<u>19/8/2013</u>

FrameWork: It is generis work(set of generic guidelines) designed by an expert and used by many people to accomplish a task in an effective,efficient and optimized way.

<u>Types of Frame Works:</u>

1. Line Frame Work.
2. Modular Frame Work.
3. Keyword Driven Frame Work.
4. Hybrid Frame Work.
5. Batch Frame Work.

Create the following Folder structure

a.Test Data.

b.Repository.

c.Library.

d.Recovery.

e.Environment.

f.Test.

g.Log.

Steps:

> ➤ Create required test data file and save them into corresponding folder.
> ➤ Create required shared repositories and save them in corresponding folder.
> ➤ Create reuired Library files and save them in corresponding folder.
> ➤ Create the required Recovery files and save them in corresponding folder.
> ➤ Create the required Environment files and save them in corresponding folder
> ➤ Open the Main test.
> ➤ Associate all the required resources.
> ➤ Develop the script in such a way that it will be executed based on the keywords specified in the datatable.
> ➤ Save the test in the corresponding folder and open it whenever we required.
> ➤ Specify the desired keys and execute it.
> ➤ Finally analyze the result.

Working with Excel Applications(without using Datatable methods):

1.Create an excel file, enter some data and save it.

Example:

Dim Excel,WorkBooks

```
Set Excel = CreateObject("Excel.Applications")

Excel.visible = true

Set WorkBooks = Excel.Workbooks.Add()

Excel.Cells(1,1).Value = "good  morning"

Escel.Cells(5,5).Value = "Happy Journey"

WorkBooks.SaveAs "d:\roopa.xls"

WorkBooks.close

Excel.Quit
```

2.Reading values from a specific Excel Sheet.

Example:

```
Dim Excel,WorkBook,WorkSheet1

Set Excel = CreateObject("Excel.Applications")

Excel.visible = true

Set WorkBook = Excel.Workbooks.Open("d:\123.xls")

Set WorkSheet1 = Excel.WorkSheets.Item("Sheet2")

Msgbox WorkSheet1.Cells(1,1).Value

Msgbox WorkSheet1.Cells(3,3).Value

WorkBook.close
```

Excel.Quit

NOTE:

Workbooks.Open Method: It is used to opening a specific Excel application.

Syntax: WorkBooks.Open ("Path of xls file")

WorkSheets.Item Method: It is used to focus on a specific escel sheet from the application.

Deleting Rows from a specific Excel Sheet:

Example:

Dim Excel,WorkBook,WorkSheet1

Set Excel = CreateObject("Excel.Applications")

Excel.visible = true

Set WorkBook = Excel.Workbooks.Open("d:\123.xls")

Set WorkSheet1 = Excel.WorkSheets.Item("Sheet2")

 WorkSheet1.Rows(1:1).Delete

 WorkSheet1.Rows(3:3).Delete

WorkBook.SaveAs("d:\NewExcel.xls")

WorkBook.close

Excel.Quit

Adding and deleting a specific Excel Sheet:

Example:

Dim Excel,WorkBook,NewSheet,DelSheet

Set Excel = CreateObject("Excel.Applications")

Excel.visible = true

Set WorkBook = Excel.Workbooks.Open("d:\123.xls")

Set NewSheet = WorkBook.Sheets.Add

NewSheet.Name = "gvg"

Set DelSheet = WorkBook.Sheets("Sheet1")

DelSheet.Delete

21/8/2013

Scenario:

In a flight reservation window, select an item from fly_from combo box and verify whether that item available or not in fly_to combo box, like this select all items one by one in fly_from combo box and verify whether that item is available or not in fly_to combo.

Window("Flight Reservation").Activate

Window("Flight Reservation").Winobject("Date of Flight:").Type "121222"

```
icount1 = Window("Flight Reservation").WinComboBox("Fly
From:").GetItemsCount()

Msbbox icount1

For I = 0 to icount1-1

Window("Flight Reservation").WinComboBox(Fly From:").Select(i)

ifrom= Window("Flight Reservation").WinComboBox("Fly
From:").GetROProperty("text")

icount2 = Window("Flight Reservation").WinComboBox("Fly
To:").GetItemsCount()

msgbox icount2

for j = 0 to icount2-1

Window("Flight Reservation").WinComboBox(Fly From:").Select(j)

ito= Window("Flight Reservation").WinComboBox("Fly
From:").GetROProperty("text")

msgbox ito

If ifrom <> ito Then

Msgbox "test passed"

Else

Msgbox "test failed"

End if
```

Next

Next

Modular FrameWork or Functional frame Decomposition:

1. Prepare individual components or each and every task.
2. Make them as reusable components.
3. Prepare the desired driver based on the end to end scenario.
4. Execute the Drivers.
5. Analyze the Results.

Actions: Action is a set of instructions to perform a specific task.

There are 2 types of actions:

1. **Normal Actions.**
2. **Reusable Actions.**

NOTE1: Reusable Actions are called in other test known as external Actions.

NOTE2: External Actions are Non-Editable.

Operations on Actions:

1. Insert a New Action.
2. Splitting an Action.
3. Making an Action as Re-usable Action.
4. Renaming an Action.
5. Calling as Existing Action.

6. Deleting an Action.

Navigation:

1.Inserting a New Action:

- ➢ Activate the menu item insert.
- ➢ Select the option insert call to new action.
- ➢ Specify the Action name.
- ➢ Click on OK.

3.Making an Action as normal action:

- ➢ Select the desired action.
- ➢ Activate the menu item edit.
- ➢ Select the action.
- ➢ Select the action properties.
- ➢ The action properties wizard will be opened.
- ➢ Specify the Action name.
- ➢ Uncheck the checkbox reusable action.

4.Renaming an Action:

- ➢ Select the required Action.
- ➢ Activate the menu item edit.
- ➢ Select Action,Rename the action.
- ➢ Specify the new action name.
- ➢ Click on OK.

6.Deleting an Action:

- ➢ Select the required action.

- ➢ Edit menu,action and delete action.

Descriptive Programming:

Without using object repository, specifying the list of main properties in the scripting itself.

Advantage:

Fast execution.

Disadvantage:

It will take more time to develop the script.

Example:

Dialog("text:=Login","x=375",).Activate

Dialog("text:=Login","x=375",).WinEdit("attached text:=AgentName:").Set "Roopa"

Dialog("text:=Login","x=375",).WinEdit("attached text:=Password:").Set Secure "******"

Dialog("text:=Login","x=375",).WinButton("text:=OK").Click

Window("text:=Flight Reservation:").Close

Exporting data from a database to textfile:

```
Dim Con,Rs,Fso,MyFile,r1,r2

Set Co = CreateObject("ADODB.Connection")

Set Rs = CreateObject("ADODB.RecordSet")

Set Fso = CreateObject("Scripting.FileSystemObject")

Set MyFile = Fso.CreateTextFile("d:\res.txt",2)

Con.Provider = "Microsoft.Jet.Oledb.4.0"

Con.Open "d:\Mydb.mdb"

Rs.Open  "Select * from Login", con

Do While not Rs.EOF

r1 = Rs.Fields("un")

r2 = Rs.Fields("pswd")

Myfile.WriteLine r1&","&r2

Rs.MoveNext

Loop
```

Recording Modes:

There are 3 types of recording modes.

1. Context/Normal recording mode.
2. Analog recording mode.
3. Low Level recording mode.

1.Normal Recording mode: It is used for recording the performed on a standard GUI objects In different situatuins.

2.Analog Recording mode: It is used for drawing and signatures.

3.Low Level recording mode: It is a special recording mode provided by QTP, which is used for recording atleast some operations on the non-supported environment also.

With this, we can generate the script and playback and we cannot modify the script.

Virtual Object Configuration: It is not a real object, but it will work like real object. Whenever the QTP not able to identify the object, then we go for virtual object configuration.

Virtual Object Manager: It is used for storing the virtual object information and also provides a provision to delete unnecessary virtual objects.

Navigation to create virtual objects:

- ➤ Activate the menu item.
- ➤ Tools, virtual objects.
- ➤ New virtual object.
- ➤ The virtual object manager wizard will be opened.
- ➤ Click on next.
- ➤ Select the object type.
- ➤ Click on next.
- ➤ Select the area with the help of mark object.
- ➤ Click on next.
- ➤ Select the parent hierarchy.
- ➤ Click on next.
- ➤ Specify the name of the button.
- ➤ Click on finish.

Regular Expressions: Whenever the object value is changing dynamically, then we will go for regular expressions.

Example:

Window("Flight Reservation:").Dialog("FaxOrderNo.*").ActiveX("MaskEdBox").Type "1111111111"

Window("Flight Reservation:").Dialog("Fax Order No.*")

WinButton("send").Click

Window("Flight Reservation:").Activate

17/9/2013

Tips for generating the basic script for web based applications.

Object/Browser
Script

Browser
>Browser("Browser Name")

Page Page("Page Name")

EditBox
>WebEdit("EditBoxName")

RadioButton
>WebRadioButton("RadioButton Name")

CheckBox
>WebCheckBox("CheckBox Name")

ListBox
>WebList("ListBox Name")

Example:

Capture the link name from the google web page and export into an text file.

NOTE:

Child objects: This method is used to capture the classname for specific object.

micclass method: This method is used to capture the name of the object.

ObjectCount: To count the number of specific objects.

```
Dim Fso,Myfile,Odesc,Lists,Nlinks

Set Fso = createobject("Scripting.FileSystemObject")

Set Myfile = Fso.CreateTextFile("d:\linknames.txt",2)

Myfile.WriteLine "linknames"

Myfile.WriteLine "*******"

Set Odesc = description.Create()

oDesc("micclass").Value = "link"

Set lists = Browser("Google").Page("Google").ChildObjects(Odesc)

Nlinks = lists.Count()

msgbox Nlinks

For i = 0 to n-1

Mylinks = lists(i).GetROProperty("text")

Myfile.WriteLine Mylinks

Next
```

Window based:

To count number of buttons in a flight reservation window.

```
Dim nbutton,buttons,tbuttons,mybuttons

Set nbutton = Description.Create

nbutton("Class Name").Value = "WinEdit"

Set buttons = Dialog("Login").ChildObjects(nbutton)

tbuttons = buttons.Count

Msgbox tbuttons

For I = 0 to tbuttons-1

Mybuttons = buttons(i).GetROProperty("text")

Msgbox mybuttons

Next
```

To appear the object in flat files

```
Dim nbutton,buttons,tbuttons,mybuttons,Fso,myfile

Set Fso = CreateObject("Scripting.FileSystemObject")

Set myfile = Fso.CreateTextFile("D:\bnames.txt",2)

myfile.WriteLine "Button Names"

myfile.WriteLine "*********"

Set nbutton = Description.Create

nbutton("Class Name").Value = "WinEdit"
```

```
Set buttons = Dialog("Login").ChildObjects(nbutton)

Tbuttons = buttons.Count

Msgbox tbuttons

For i = 0 to tbuttons-1

mybuttons = buttons(i).GetROProperty("text")

myfile.WriteLine mybuttons

Next
```

Input and Output Parameters:

```
VbWindow("Form1").VbEdit("Text1").Set parameter("v1")

VbWindow("Form1").VbEdit("Text2").Set parameter("v2")

VbWindow("Form1").VbButton("ADD").Click

res1 = VbWindow("Form1").VbEdit("Text3").GetROProperty("text")

parameter("a") = res1

VbWindow("Form1").VbButton("SUB").Click

res2 = VbWindow("Form1").VbEdit("Text3").GetROProperty("text")

parameter("b") = res2

VbWindow("Form1").VbButton("MUL").Click
```

res3 = VbWindow("Form1").VbEdit("Text3").GetROProperty("text")

parameter("c") = res3

Navigation:

1.Go to new test.

2.Insert →Call to existing action

RunAction "Action1[Res]", oneIteration,100,200,a,b,c

Msgbox a

Msgbox b

Msgbox c

*Verify the order no. in the flight reservation window and check whether the order is accepting only numerical values or not.

Window("Flight Reservation").Activate

Window("Flight Reservation").WinMenu("Menu").Select "File;Open Order…"

Window("Flight Reservation").Dialog("OpenOrder").WinCheckbox("orderno.").Set "ON"

Window("Flight Reservation").Dialog("Openorder").WinEdit("Edit").Set "Nellore"

```
ord = Window("Flight
Reservation").Dialog("openorder").WinEdit("Edit").GetROProperty("tex
t")
If ord = "Nellore" Then
Msgbox "test failed"
Else
Msgbox "test passed"

End If
```

Automation Object Model: It is a collection of objects, methods and properties , which are used to perform operations on the Quick Test Professional.

Scenario: Open the QTP and open a new test

Dim qtApp

Set qtApp = CreateObject("QuickTest.Application")

If qtApp.Launched <> True then

qtApp.Launch

End if

qtApp.Visible = true

qtApp.New

*Opent the Quick Test Professional and minimize and maximize

Dim qtApp

Set qtApp = CreateObject("QuickTest.Application")

```
If qtApp.Launched <> True then

qtApp.Launch

End if

qtApp.Visible = true

qtApp.New

qtApp.WindowState = "maximized"

qtApp.WindowState = "minimized"
```

*Start the QTP, opening an existing test.

```
Dim qtApp

Set qtApp = CreateObject("QuickTest.Application")

If qtApp.Launched <> True then

qtApp.Launch

End if

qtApp.Visible = true

qtApp.New

qtApp.WindowState = "maximized"

qtApp.WindowState = "minimized"

qtApp.Open "path of the file"
```

*Using crypt.Encrypt method: It is a utility object provided by QTP, which is used for generating the encrypted password.

Example:

Dim pass

Pass = "Roopa"

Msgbox Crypt.Encrypt(pass)

---> **Using password encoder:** This is the tool provided by QTP, to encode the password.

Navigation: All programs→Hp Quick Test Professional→ under the tools→password encoder

NOTE: Why the password encoder is required?

In the most of the automation project, the script would be dealing the usernames and passwords. Many of the cases, the automation script would be maintained by multiple people or by multiple team members. In such situations, the encrypt password is used, so that the original password are exposed unnecessarily.

Important VbScript functions:

1. **Abs(Absolute) Function:** It returns the absolute values of a number.

Example: DimVal

Val = abs(-50.33)

Msgbox Val

2. **Left Function:** It returns the left side characters from the original string.

Example: Dim Val, Mystring

Mystring = "QTPTraining"

Val = Left(MyString,3)

Msgbox Val

3. **Right Function:** It returns the right side characters from the string.

Example: Dim Val,Mystring

Mystring = "QTPTraining"

Val = Right(Mystring,8)

Msgbox Val

4. **Len Function:** It returns the number of characters in a string.

Example: Dim Mystring

Mystring = Inputbox("Enter the string:")

Mystring = Len(Mystring)

Msgbox Mystring

5. **Time Function:** It returns the current system time.

Example: Dim MyTime

MyTime = Time

Msgbox MyTime

6. **Join Function:** It returns a string created by joining a number of strings, contained in an array.

Example: Dim Mystring,MyArray(2)

MyArray(0) = "Welcome"

MyArray(1) = "To India"

Mystring = Join(MyArray)

Msgbox Mystring

7. **Hour Function:** It returns the number between 0 and 23, representing the hour of the day.

Example: Dim Mytime,Myhour

Mytime Now

Myhour = hour(Mytime)

Msgbox Myhour

8. **Now Function:** It returns the current system date and time.

Example: Dim Mytime

Mytime = Now

Msgbox Mytime

9. **Asc Function:** It returns the ANSI characters from a letter.

Example: Dim Mynum

Mynum = Asc("D")

Msgbox Mynum

10. **Inputbox Function:** It displays the prompt in a dialog box for providing the input values from the user.

Reporter.ReportEvent: This is a utility object provided by QTP, which is used for generating the user defined result in the result window.

Condition1: Read a mobile number and verify the series, if its starts with 9866 or 9966, then it displays a airtel mobile number.

Condition2: If its starts with 9440 or 9441, then it displays mobile number.

Nested If statement: Nested If statement is where you can have, an if statement within an If statement.

Example:

Dim Val, Val_length, Val_Numeric, Val_Series, Val_Start

Val = Inputbox("enter the mobile number:")

Val_length = Len(Val)

```
Val_Numeric = IsNumeric(Val)

Val_Starts = Left(Val,1)

Val_Series = Left(Val,4)

If Val_length = 10 and Val_Starts = 9 Then

If Val_Series = 9866 or Val_Series = 9866 Then

Msgbox "It is a airtel number"

Else If Val_Series = 9440 or Val_Series = 9441 Then

Msgbox "It is a BSNL number"

End If

End If

End If
```

*Write a program to find out whether the given number is even or odd.

```
Dim val

val = inputbox("enter the value:")

If val Mod 2 = 0 Then

Msgbox "even number"
```

Else

Msgbox "odd number"

End If

*Read two numbers and display their sum.

Dim num1,num2,tot

num1 = inputbox("enter num1 value:")

num2 = inputbox("enter num2 value:")

tot = cdbl(num1)+cdbl(num2)

msgbox tot

{cdbl = convert to double}

{cint = convert string to integer}

*Read four subject marks and calculate the total and grade.

Condition1: If average marks greater than or equal to 75, grade is distinction.

Condition2: If average marks are >=60 and <75 then grade is first class.

Condition3: If average marks >=50 and <60 then grade is second class.

Condition4: If average marks >=40 and <50 then grade is third class.

Condition5: Minimum marks should be 40 in any subject otherwise grade is fail.

```
Dim sqtp,slr,sqc,ssql,tot

sqtp = inputbox("enter qtp marks:")

slr = inputbox("enter loadrunner marks:")

sqc = inputbox("enter quality center marks:")

ssql = inputbox("enter sql marks:")

tot = cint(sqtp)+cint(slr)+cint(sqc)+cint(ssql)

Msgbox tot

If cdbl(sqtp)>=40 and cdbl(slr)>=40 and cdbl(ssql)>=40 and
cdbl(sqc)>=40 and cdbl(tot)>= 300 Then

Msgbox "grade is distinction"

Else if cdbl(tot)>=240 and cdbl(tot)<300 then

Msgbox "grade is first class")

Else if cdbl(tot)>=200 and cdbl(tot)<240 then

Msgbox "grade is second class"

Else if cdbl(tot)>=160 and cdbl(tot)<200 then

Msgbox "grade is third class"

Else msgbox "grade is fail"

End If
```

*Display the natural numbers upto 'n' and capture the result into an text file.

Dim fso,num,n,myfile

n = inputbox("enter the value:")

num = 1

For num = 1 to n

set fso = CreateObject("Scripting.FileSystemObject")

set myfile = fso.OpenTextFile("d:\123.txt",2)

myfile.WriteLine num

Next

* Display the natural numbers upto 'n' in reverse and capture the result into an text file.

Dim fso,num,n,myfile

n = inputbox("enter the value:")

num = 1

For num = 1 to n step-1

set fso = CreateObject("Scripting.FileSystemObject")

set myfile = fso.OpenTextFile("d:\123.txt",2)

myfile.WriteLine num

Next

*In a google web page get the collection of child objects of object class.

NOTE: From every child object properties capture the following.

1. html tag
2. inner text
3. href

Example:

Dim desobj,objcoll,objcount,i

Set desobj = Description.Create()

desobj("micclass").Value = "link"

Set objcoll = Browser("IRCTC Online Passenger").Page("IRCTC Online Passenger").Childobjects(desobj)

objcount = objcoll.count

msgbox objcount

Datatable.Addsheet "Roopa"

Datatable.ImportSheet "D:\roopa1.xls",1,3

Datatable.Getsheet(3)

For I = 0 to objcount-1

```
Datatable.SetCurrentRow(+1)

Datatable.Value("html tag",3)= objcoll(i).GetROProperty("html tag")

Datatable.Value("innertext",3)= objcoll(i).GetROProperty("innertext")

Datatable.Value("href",3)= objcoll(i).GetROProperty("href")

Next

Datatable.Value.ExportSheet "D:\Roopa1.xls",3
```

*Invoke the QTP, opening an existing test, associate all the object repositories and save the text using automation object model (AOM).

```
Dim qtapp,qttest,qtrepositories

Set qtapp = createobject("QuickTest.Application")

If qtapp.Launched<> true Then

qtapp.Launch

End If

qtapp.Visible = true

qtapp.Open "C:\Documents and settings\Admin\Desktop\Login",False

Set qtrepositories = qtapp.test.Actions("Action1").ObjectRepositories

If qtrepositories.Find ("C:\Documents and settings\Admin\Desktop\Login.tsr") = true Then

qtrepositories.Add "C:\Documents and settings\Admin\Desktop\Login.tsr",1

End If

qtapp.Test.Run

qtapp.Test.Save

qtapp.Quit
```

Static method: This method is used to capture the static property from the application.

Example: In login dialog box, verify the help message(The message is mercury(password message))

Dim imsg

Dialog("Login").Activate

Dialog("Login").WinButton("Help").Click

imsg = Dialog("Login").Dialog("Flight Reservation").Static("The password is 'MERCURY'").GetROProperty("text")

If imsg = "The password is 'MERCURY'") Then

Msgbox "correct password"

Else

Msgbox "wrong password"

End If

Menu Object: This method will work only for windows based applications.

Default method for menu option is "**select**"

Example:

*From a notepad get the menu list names and get the menu item names from the menu

1. Get the menu list names.

Dim cnt,n,ipath

Cnt = Window("Notepad").WinMenu("Menu").GetItemProperty("","SubMenuCount")

For n = 1 to cnt

Ipath = Window("Notepad").WinMenu("Menu").BuildMenuPath(itempath,n)

Msgbox ipath

Msgbox Window("Notepad").WinMenu("Menu").GetItemProperty(ipath,"Label")

Next

2.Get the menu item names

Dim cnt,n,ipath

Cnt = Window("Notepad").WinMenu("Menu").GetItemProperty("File","SubMenuCount")

For n = 1 to cnt

Ipath = Window("Notepad").WinMenu("Menu").BuildMenuPath(File,n)

Msgbox ipath

```
Msgbox
Window("Notepad").WinMenu("Menu").GetItemProperty(ipath,"Label
")

Next
```

12/10/2013

*Capture the link name in a google page and capture into an excel file (without using data driven method).

```
Dim iexcel,objdesc,objcall,sname,isheet,iworkbook

Set iexcel = CreateObject("Excel.Application")

Set iworkbook = iexcel.ActiveWorkbook

iexcel.Visible = true

iexcel.Workbooks.Add

Set isheet = iexcel.ActiveSheet

Set objdesc = Description.Create

objdesc("micclass").Value = "Link"

Set objcoll = Browser("IRCTC Online Passenger").Page("IRCTC Online
Passenger").ChildObjects(objdesc)

Msgbox objcoll.count

For i = 0 to objcoll.count-1
```

```
sname = objcoll(i).GetROProperty("text")

Isheet.Cells(i+1,1) = sname

Wait(5)

Next

Set iworkbook = iexcel.ActiveWorkbook

iworkbook.SaveAs "D:\IRCTCLinks.xls"

iexcel.Quit
```

Transaction: It is a new concept provided by QTP 9.5, it is used to calculate the response time. It can be divided into 2 types.

1. **Start Transaction.**
2. **End Transaction.**

Syntax: Services.StartTransaction "Transaction Name"

  Statements to be executed

Services.End Transaction

Step Generator: With the help of step generator, manually, we can generate the basic script lines.

NOTE: shortcut key F7